When Life, Not Death, Do us Part

Keabecoe Choene

Published by Family House Publishers (Pty) Ltd, 2020.

WHEN LIFE, NOT DEATH, DO US PART

First edition. December 15, 2020.

Copyright © 2020 Keabecoe Choene.

ISBN: 979-8224328475

Written by Keabecoe Choene.

Table of Contents

Dedication

Dedications

The book is dedicated to

My Family

This is a classic example of our pain becoming a purposeful book. This has been one of the things that God used to bring us closer. Will I have chosen it to be this way? Not in my wildest dreams. Was it worth it? A gigantic "Yes!" Only because it brought me face to face with the Almighty God who gave me a second chance. Divorce does not only affect the couple, but families are affected as well. As you watched my lowest moments in life, I saw a light of hope in you. I am grateful for the love and support you gave me.

Every Divorcee

Nobody gets married to divorce, unless they are twisted and wicked. When I was married, I wish someone would have told me that it gets better, it can be healed and it can be worked out; but no one did, only because we never searched hard enough and did not turn all stones.

When I went through the divorce, no one shared how painful it would be. Divorcees always splashed a "great life after divorce" image and when I did not get my great-after story, I was shattered. I only found my greatest comfort in Jesus.

This is the time to remove your focus from yourself and your failed marriage and focus on Jesus Christ. He is the best in dealing with the broken pieces of your heart and life. Life does not end because your marriage did. There are so many things you have not done and explored. Now is that time. You can begin your new journey, and that journey becomes a fruitful one when you take it with Him. May you find your purpose in Him; for we were made for His pleasure.

When Life,
Not Death,
Do Us Part

This book belongs to

Malachi 2: 16 "For I hate divorce!" says the Lord God of Israel. "To divorce

your wife is to overwhelm her with cruelty, "says the Lord of Heaven's

Armies. "So, guard your heart; do not be unfaithful to your wife." (NLT)

Matthew 19:6 "Wherefore they are no more twain, but one lesh.

What therefore God hath joined together, let no man put asunder

Published by Shimmy C. Kotu for

Family House Publishers (Pty) Ltd
P.O. Box 21994, Helderkruin, 1733, Republic of South Africa
www.shimmykotu.com
www.familyhouse.co.za
chi@shimmykotu.com

Typesetting and Graphic Design by
Kyle Mabaso for
CDE Insight (Pty) Ltd.
www.cdeinsight.co.za

About the Author

Mom to Choaro Nahum Osei.

Daughter to Ivy Emily Choene.

Sister to Will, Tsholofelo, MacDonald and Moipone.

Aunt to Abongile, Will II and Naledi.

The highest calling for her is being a servant and follower of Jesus Christ.

She is saved by grace and loves much, because she has been forgiven much.

She is a Jesus gal through and through.

She serves the Master who gave His life for hers; the Master who requires nothing less than her life. She surrendered her life to live for His glory. She spends that life pursuing, serving and doing what her Master commands. In Him she lives, she moves and has her being.

She believes that if you love Him, you will tell others about Him, because in the end it is all about Him.

Dedications

The book is dedicated to

My Family

This is a classic example of our pain becoming a purposeful book. This has been one of the things that God used to bring us closer. Will I have chosen it to be this way? Not in my wildest dreams. Was it worth it? A gigantic "Yes!" Only because it brought me face to face with the Almighty God who gave me a second chance. Divorce does not only affect the couple, but families are affected as well. As you watched my lowest moments in life, I saw a light of hope in you. I am grateful for the love and support you gave me.

Every Divorcee

Nobody gets married to divorce, unless they are twisted and wicked. When I was married, I wish someone would have told me that it gets better, it can be healed and it can be worked out; but no one did, only because we never searched hard enough and did not turn all stones.

When I went through the divorce, no one shared how painful it would be. Divorcees always splashed a "great life after divorce" image and when I did not get my great-after story, I was shattered. I only found my greatest comfort in Jesus.

This is the time to remove your focus from yourself and your failed marriage and focus on Jesus Christ. He is the best in dealing with the broken pieces of your heart and life. Life does not end because your marriage did. There are so many things you have not done and explored. Now is that time. You can begin your new journey, and that journey becomes a fruitful one when you take it with Him. May you find your purpose in Him; for we were made for His pleasure.

Naming of the Book

The initial title of the book was "To Divorce or Not to Divorce." That changed, because I realised how emotional the book became once the writing began. The title of the book is derived from a biblical perspective where the Bible shares the truth that God hates divorce - how shocking is that truth though.

It is challenging to imagine "God" and "hate" mentioned in the same sentence. Isn't it amazing that though we know God hates all sin, His Word still emphasizes that He particularly hates divorce? Not only is divorce sin, but God had to get it in our hearts and minds that He hates it.

Malachi 2:16-17 'For the man who does not love his wife but divorces her', says the Lord, the God of Israel, 'covers his garment with violence', says the Lord of hosts. 'So, guard yourself in your spirit and do not be faithless.'

Actually, that Malachi chapter has some rough analogy on why He hates divorce. Read it and it shall enlighten you.

There is so much that the church debates on the topic of divorce. There is so much debate and hostility around this topic that the church ends up neglecting those that are hurting because of going through divorce. Christians really do battle with the question of divorce - whether this question is posed to friends or in their Christian circles, and to colleagues or in their private thoughts. The question, "to divorce or not to" does come up even to the most devoted of God's children.

I toyed with that title, secondly because even non-Christians are having the same debate in their circles. Others ask such when they are faced with certain hardships and tribulations, situation and circumstance. I have lost count of how often I have asked myself this question while I was still married.

Thirdly, the "to divorce or not to divorce' title was a lingering thought in my mind, because it is derived from a nagging question I have always had - is divorce really the answer or worth the effort and its aftermath?

The question itself indicates how conflicted the individual asking the question could be. Sometimes we could be so overwhelmed by our own situation that we are blinded from seeing things clearly. So, conversations arise with either ourselves or with others regarding our relationship.

After a long consideration, I finally settled for the book title – "When Life, Not Death, Do Us Apart."

Introduction

When I had my son, I came across the "many things that mothers never share with you" type of scenarios. It is the same with getting divorced. The divorced make it seem so easy and free. No one ever tells you the other side of the fence until you have to personally climb over it. Later in the book, I shall share a little about the divorce aftermath from my personal experience, which shall be about the emotional, spiritual, social, material changes and dynamics no one would have ever prepared me for. These changes, though different from one individual to the other, do nonetheless come and ultimately change the person you were before the divorce.

I am in no way advocating for divorce, yet the reality is that many go through it with little or no support at all. I consider myself blessed, because I had friends and family who supported me. The reality is, even if the whole world rallies around you, it is still something that you need to get over by yourself, mostly because it hits you so much inside. It knocks down your dream of "forever" and shakes off your belief of growing old with someone. You suddenly have to deal with the reality that was never a part of your plans.

No one gets married to get divorced. Who wants to do that to their hearts? So, when we say "I do", we hope that it is forever and when forever is suddenly not part of the equation, a new future and new plans have to be forged and made. This process takes some longer than others to map out and actualize, with very few ever making the transition productively. Divorce is hard and harsh; hence I wrote this book for someone to have an understanding of what they are about to go through.

I did not think the pain would ever end. I did not think the humiliation would ever stop. I did not think that the sadness and confusion would ever end. I went out looking for a book I could read to regain some hope, but I did not get any.

Truth is, any book can inform you, but only the Bible can transform you. So, I had no choice but to turn to it. God in His infinite power used so many people to cross paths with me to lead me to a place of healing. Some hurt me; others caused me pain, but most encouraged me immensely. I could not have gotten through this time without my family, friends, Moruti Shimmy and Mama Mercy Kotu. At the time of my deepest hurt, they embraced me with love and wrapped me around with prayer. I don't know how much I have called, messaged and cried to Pastor Shimmy and Mama Mercy; and all of those times I was never rejected or neglected.

Families of those going through divorce don't know what to say and friends don't even know what to do. Some people think when the divorce is over in court or on a piece of paper, it will also be over in your heart. They think that just because it is over in court you are supposed to be already over it; but most of the time it is then that you begin to deal with a lot of conflicting, confusing and often frustrating emotions and thoughts.

God took me through my own path and since His plans are never the same for everyone, I pray that if you are going through a divorce, you will find God's love, forgiveness, grace, mercy, strength, wisdom and comfort.

This is my story, but I can assure you now that He has a plan for you to recognize and walk through. As you read a bit of my story, I pray that you look up towards the heavens, because that is where your help will come from. He loves you so much that He is waiting to receive your broken heart and broken life so He can do something wonderful with them. It is when we search for Him that we find ourselves.

Isaiah 1:18 reads, "Come now, let us reason together, says the Lord. Though your sins are like scarlet, they shall be white as snow. Though they are red like crimson, they shall become like wool."

Divorce Equals Death

Divorce is probably the closest thing to death. It feels like a ripping out of your soul while you still live. When I was married, I never fully understood the concept of oneness. I gave him my body, exchanged my name for his and gave my life to be with him forever; but "oneness" was a concept I had not yet grasped. It was in the process of divorce that oneness became a vivid reality to me.

You do feel like a significant part was ripped from your soul. It feels like a part of you is no longer there somehow. It's almost like you are exposed and your soul is lying there bare and uncovered. Divorce, unlike death, lacks a sense of closure and finality.

I lost my biological father years back and I did not attend his funeral. Even though I knew he was no longer around, I lacked a sense of closure; because there was no funeral memory to always go back to. There was a sense of loss, but the finality of it all is something I will never ever have. That is the reason those who have their family members die at war, or those who lost their beloved abroad during the anti-apartheid struggle have a hard time finding closure. A funeral and a body give the soul and spirit the element of finality. You see, with death, even though you can be in denial, the inevitable is fast approaching - there will be an actual ceremony. You know there shall be an actual funeral which you have to be a part of. Notwithstanding how you feel, there shall be a place, time and event where your loved one will be laid to rest.

I remember my late aunt who was the closest thing to a mother to me. When she passed on, I was devastated and when the day of the funeral came, I was deeply sad. I remember crying and not being able to stop myself. I was still lost after her death ("lost" is the only word I can use right now, because I can't find a proper word in my limited vocabulary). Though I felt lost, and it took time for me to accept and live without her; there was, nonetheless closure, because I stood over her grave and saw her body lowered into the ground.

With divorce, it is a different matter. Your beloved is no longer with you and might not even want to be with you ever again. It feels like they are dead, but they are not. As soon as you get accustomed to living without them, you meet them and they can call you, especially if you have children together. So, not only are you harassed by constant memories of a once strong bond, the living evidence of its death still walks around. So, they are dead to you; or at least you want them to be, but they are not, and because of the non-closure or finality that is so characteristic of all divorces, you are forced to deal with the pain, emptiness and loss afresh daily.

Divorce is confrontational. It is in your face daily. You get to be asked about your ex regularly. Letters could still be delivered to your house. Mail and accounts could still come to you with their names on them. As much as you want to leave the past behind, divorce can't be left behind. It is everywhere. It is in the restaurant you used to frequent and in the house you once shared. For some peculiar reason, your child starts resembling the one who left, because your child is another constant living reminder of the divorce.

Just like death, you must mourn your divorce. Don't think it is just, "By the way I am leaving." No Ma'am; no Sir. Those vows got you entangled with your ex-spouse to an extent far greater than any physical bond or child could. They joined you together! They made you one! Your vows were not only between the two of you, but you were joined together before friends, family and most importantly, God. Family and friends were witnesses and more frightening is the fact that God was also a witness. He says so in Malachi 2:14.

You must mourn and mourn completely. What do I mean with "mourn completely"? Divorce has several stages, phases and emotions. This is what I want us to share in this book - the different phases or emotions that I went through while going through the divorce. These phases or emotions can come at different times for different people.

This book is definitely not a cure for anything. It is just a light for someone who is going through the dark tunnel of divorce. Some people feel like their whole world is falling apart during the divorce. I certainly felt like that. You feel like your life is over and you will never live again. Well, this book is to let you know that you will live again and life is not over.

When I got divorced, I felt alone, even with my life full of people; even with the house full of people. As much as your family and friends are wishing you well, some might not even have the faintest idea of what you are going through; and if you belong to the church fraternity, you are even denied to feel anything, because faith is perceived by some to be a magic spell that wipes away all ill feelings and sorrow.

Though some spouses know deep down that their marriage was always in trouble, there is something about getting divorce summons or order which drives the wounds even deeper and makes the reality of life apart as inevitable as the sunrise - it is here, whether we feel like getting up or not, and you have to deal with it. There is also the myth that the one who initiated the divorce is heartless and hurting less than the defendant. Well contrary to popular belief, they too hurt as deeply. No one can ever predict how we will all react, especially in a divorce situation. You once stood before family, friends and God to profess your love and forsook all to cling to each other; yet now you want out? That in itself feels like a ton of bricks falling on you.

I will always remember my first lawyer's consultation. Since then, I have gone through a lot of visits until I lost count, but will never forget my first consultation. I was so confused, but I wanted to stop the pain and mostly the humiliation and disrespect I was feeling then.

Prior to that visit, I had tried all I knew then to save my marriage, but had ultimately resolved this divorce would be the best option. Well as I sat there, I never could have imagined what was coming. You have to remember that this is a lawyer who probably thinks you have thought this through before coming to see him. Well, he was wrong. But then you ask yourself, "How does he perceive me? Am I only his next meal or a person in need of his professional services?"

I sat there and he gave me forms to fill out after a few questions. What struck me was the form from Statistic SA one fills in the lawyer's office. As awkward as that meeting was, how painful, dreadful and lost I felt. All I could think of was, "God, how could I be a statistic? How did I get here?" I sat there and thought, "The next time I hear someone say 'in South Africa, 10 in 50 couples get a divorce', they will be referring to me." I was deeply troubled by being a statistic than anything else. Yes, I was scared that my ex would freak out at discovering that I had instituted divorce proceedings, but I knew deep down he would not be utterly surprised at all. If he was surprised, that would surprise me indeed.

As I walked away from that office, I knew it was over. The dream of "forever together" was over. It was dead with no prospects of resurrection. For the first time ever in my life, (though I had multiple previous relationship heartbreaks) I felt like a failure. I felt unlovable, unloved, and useless. I so felt like dying.

Here is my word of advice - If you are trusting God for the restoration of your marriage, stay far away from lawyers and courts. They create an illusion of hopelessness. I always tell people that if I did not have a son, I don't think I would have ever wanted to live. I so wanted to die. The only reason I wanted to live was because I could not stand anyone else raising him. I could not stand not seeing him grow up.

At home I was always the strong one, the one who got a lot done with minimal resources, yet and for the first time ever, I compared myself with my siblings and realized that I was falling apart. I could not stand being helpless. I have always considered myself a strong woman who for the rest of her life always commanded respect. I did not think I ever needed a man for anything, but here I was falling apart because of a man. Now I felt powerless, worthless, and completely lost. So, while filling those divorce papers, I was not on top of the world and sipping some bubbly drink (never mind the fact that I don't drink alcohol). I was not celebrating when I got back. I was not relieved; instead I was terrified, confused and alone. I knew that the way life was, it would never ever be again. I filed for divorce, because I thought that if I did not, I would never have lived long.

So, the next few pages will reveal phases and emotions that I went through when facing divorce. I wrote what I felt going through my divorce, not as a book but as a coping mechanism. I documented my own feelings just to keep check of my own thoughts in an attempt to unravel them. I wished there was a book I could have read when I was going through my divorce, but there was none. I felt that no one understood what I was going through.

I had to trust that God knew and understood what I was going through. I read the book of Psalms from the Bible a lot and the words that held me together during this ordeal came from Psalms 46:10, which reads, "Be still and know that I am God."

Though I could not do much, I had to be still and know that He is God.

Hurt

At the beginning of a divorce, you feel a lot of emotions. During mine, I certainly oscillated between hurt and betrayal; a hurt so deep to your soul it can't be explained verbally. It's the type of emotion that only those who experienced it will know what I am describing. How do you explain a headache to someone who has never had one before?

Some people are led to the lawyers by that pain. That pain pierces and cuts very deep. It blinds you to a point that you can't see the future with this individual anymore. This type of pain whispers to the soul that there is no going forward as long as you are together. When one contemplates divorce, I always advise them to talk to someone and talk to them extensively, because a lot of us made that decision based on the pain without thinking through some pertinent post-divorce realities.

Had some of us gone to someone who gave us a glimpse of hope for a better future with our spouses, we would not have divorced. That is the reason it matters who you confide in when you are contemplating divorce. Please do not talk to yourself and make the final decision based on the outcomes of self-talk. Go for professional counselling. Go to people who have been married for decades. Go to the elders in your family and you will find that someone somewhere "got over" what you perceive to be the highest mountain or deepest valley. In seeking solutions to your marital crisis, impasse or dilemma, don't leave any stone unturned.

The initial pain is intense. When asked why you want to get a divorce, all you point at is the bad and the ugly, as you can't even see any good with your spouse at that point; none whatsoever. That is the reason someone else's perspective could be of much help to you. I remember in the course of my divorce, when the summons was served, I signed for it and immediately went outside. Someone realized I was fazed and started sharing a story of how my husband had done them good. All I could think of was, "Who are they talking about, because it is certainly not my estranged husband." At this point, you only see red; nothing else. You only see the bad they have done to you, nothing else.

Never believe the initial feelings ever! Please note this fact - don't let your pain pile up or accumulate. Pray and talk to the Holy Spirit always about what you are going through and how it makes you feel.

Do not let the hurt inform how you generally perceive your spouse, because truth is, they may have done great things for you before the divorce, be it during your dating or marriage. The good they could have done for you in the past can't seem to come up to the surface once we are thinking of divorce.

We never generally hear wives contemplating divorce say, "My husband put me through school", or hear any husband say, "My wife gave me money to start my business." Ask anyone going through a divorce and you shall be immediately confronted with convenient amnesia regarding the good their estranged spouses did them. For the life of me, I too could not remember the good he had done. Looking back, sometimes you think the bad far outweighs the good.

SO, SITTING IN THAT lawyer's office, I was devastated. My hurt was bigger than the Kimberly Big Hole. I had left my matrimonial home to go and live at my mom's and for three months he did not come even once to at least beg me to return home. There was no text of how much he missed me, and there was no "I am miserable without you, please let's work on our marriage." So, I was utterly and deeply hurt. I was disappointed that the one I willingly gave my heart and life to, did not love me enough to care if I left or stayed.

Him not fetching me hurt even more and confirmed what my head had always known - maybe I was not loved. A knife with the longest blade would be too short to cause the hurt I felt. No sword would be long enough to inflict more pain. I was devastated! It cut deep! Never had I ever experienced deeper pain. I had my heart broken before, but this one was more devastating. It felt like I would never get over it. The one who promised me "forever" now wanted nothing to do with me.

I remember having a conversation with my older brother, who is by the way my super hero, and he told me he would go to any extent to recapture his wife's interest, attention and love. That was how much he loved her. He said he would be willing to beg and persuade her to return to him. It is at that point that I realized that not only was I not loved enough to be pursued, I probably never was. With the truth staring me in the face, I had to accept that the one I thought would fight to keep me, did not find me worth it. I was hurt and humiliated. It hurt and it did deeply.

I knew I had to step away with the little dignity that I thought I still had left. I could not beg him to love me and I could not imagine living in a house with someone who detested me. I could not beg him to stay either. So, my meeting with the lawyers happened in the midst of all of the confusion, hurt, humiliation and pain. What further exacerbated the matter was that while I grieved over our failing marriage, he was busy posting pictures of himself and his PA on social media. Of course, this added to my pain. I could no longer avoid the reality of our imminent marital demise.

For years I had to deal with the PA being thrown in my face. Now they had unapologetically ventured into the public domain. There was no stopping the man. It was clear where his heart was. So, I had to pack and go, even though that was the last thing I ever wanted to do. I had preached to women to fight in prayer for their marriages, but when this happened to me, I had no prayer energy left in me. I had prayed for so long, yet, instead of repenting and making amends, he was digressing further. With every year that went by, we drifted further apart. So, I figured that before we hurt each other more, I would have to end the ordeal.

I must admit though that when I reflect on it, I only realize now that I could not trust God with my pain. In my frustrated mind I reasoned that the pain was mine and there was no way He could deal with it. I reasoned that, after all, I gave God my husband to change, but that never happened. It is true that we always want to change our partners. As soon as we fall in love with them, we want to change them, and when the anticipated change is not forthcoming, we blame them and God; not ourselves.

My eyes were not even opened yet to God's Sovereignty, so I was a blind sheep walking along following my own instincts. I was hurt. I did not even realize how hurt I was until I had to deal with the pain. In praying for our spouses, we never realize how we could be the ones needing the change; hence we do not take ourselves to the Master for change; preferring rather to take others.

You see, the fruit of the spirit is not projecting our expectations at others, but that which needs to manifest in us. The hardest man to change is the one who thinks they do not need to change. The hardest man to change is the one looking back at us in that mirror.

Our deepest pain could be self-inflicted, yet we blame those around us, because it is easier to do so than to admit that we are the one who need to change.

Anger

After much hurt, anger flooded my emotions. My emotions oscillated between hurt and anger, as is usually the case with couples going through a divorce. The plaintiff and the defendant go through these emotions all the time as they begin to reflect on their failing or collapsing marriage. People get angry that they were served papers at work where they hold respectable positions and are known to be outstanding workers. So, they could move from anger to embarrassment, because it is in our selfish nature to care more about our image and reputation than our hurting spouses.

I want to mention though that there are extremely inhumane ways of serving a summons. For an example, someone just had sex with their spouse before leaving for work and later that very day they get served a summons at their workplace. Some live in the same house in seeming peace without any expression of grief by either spouse when out of nowhere there is a messenger at the door with a divorce summons.

Considering the modern-day culture of divorce-on-demand, I think one should not be surprised at all when one gets a divorce summons from an outwardly happy spouse. In all honesty, if I slept with you or had sex with you in the morning and in the afternoon at work, I get divorce papers, how am I supposed to feel? Would my anger be unjustifiable? I would personally be extremely angry and confused. I would be thinking, between the kisses and hugs, could you not at least not have mentioned that it was over between us?

I think the troubled couple should get to a stage where they have tried all they could to save their marriage, that getting a divorce summons is not a surprise, because they both knew that day would come. Even if I knew my spouse wanted to divorce me, do you know how it feels like to get those papers? In my case, I initiated the divorce proceedings which dragged on for a while until lawyers withdrew from the case, after which my husband went and revived the process. So, I know how it feels like to be on both sides of the wall, as I have served and have been served; with my summons coming through E-mail and his served at the office. Upon receiving his, I felt truly betrayed, because when there was a suspension in the divorce process I initiated, I thought we had a chance to work on our marriage, only to be hit with a double whammy.

When he revived the divorce, he said he had moved on and wanted closure. So, imagine your own husband telling you that he is seeing someone else and wants to be with her and not you! Holy anger right there! I kept it together in his presence, but my heart was cut into a million pieces and there seemed to be no means of mending it. I was angry at what he did to us. I was angry at what he was about to put us through. I remember thinking, "We have a son; did he even consider him at all?"

I was angry and furious at him for breaking our home. I was not as such angry at him for serving me a divorce summons as I was at him going to the extent of deciding it was the only solution. I was furious! I was thinking, "How dare you? After all we have been through, were all our love, endurance, care and commitment worth nothing at all?" I was angry that he had lied to me when he said our love would be forever! He had lied, betrayed me and betrayed us; and I was angry. I could not for the life of me understand how he could think this was better. I sent him angry messages, which he just read and never responded to. That really aggravated my anger. I would think, "How dare you ignore me?" My anger reloaded. I would often send him very long and emotional messages, to which he would respond by a simple, "Ok!" At that point, my anger knew no bounds. I would think, "This man's mission is to infuriate me."

Anger can lead you to make rash, and irrational decisions which can sabotage and abort your destiny. Please do not make permanent decisions when you are angry; never! You see, there is something about focusing on us rather on Christ that makes us powerless. Anger does exactly that. Colossians 3:8 (ESV) reads, "Now you must put these all away: anger, wrath, malice, slander, and obscene talk from your mouth." Anger is nothing to be proud of. That is the reason God tells us to put it away. So, why hold on to it? Put it away immediately!

Deuteronomy 34:1-7 (ESV) reads, "Then Moses went up from the plains of Moab to mount Nebo, to the top of Pisgah, which is opposite Jericho. And the Lord showed him all the land, Gilead as far as Dan, all Naphtali, the land of Ephraim and Manassas, all the land of Judah as far as the western sea, the Negev, and the Plain, that is, the Valley of Jericho the city of Palm trees as far as Zoar. And the Lord said to him, "This is the land of which I swore to Abraham, to Isaac, and to Jacob, "I will give it to your offspring." I have let you see it with your eyes, but shall not go over there. So, Moses, the servant of the Lord died there in the land of Moab, according to the word of the Lord and he buried him in the Valley in the land of Moab opposite Beth-peor, but no one knows the place of his burial to this day. Moses was 120 years old when he does. His eye was undimmed and his vigour unabated."

Moses failed to enter Canaan, because in his moment of anger at the Israelites, he despised and disobeyed God by hitting the rock twice, instead of pointing at it as God had commanded. Here is the account of that fateful day in Moses' life -

Numbers 20:2-12 (ESV) "Now there was no water for congregation, and they assembly themselves against Aaron. And the people quarreled with Moses and said "Would that we had perished before Lord! Why have you brought the assembly of the Lord into this wilderness, that we should die here, both we our cattle? And why have you made us come up out of Egypt to bring us to this evil place? It is no place for train or figs or vines or pomegranates and there is no water to drink.

Then Moses and Aaron went from the presence of the assembly to tent of meeting and fell on their faces. And the glory of the Lord spoke to them, and the Lord appeared to them, and the Lord spoke to Moses, saying "Take the staff and assemble the congregation, you and Aaron your brother and tell the rock before their eyes to yield its water. So, you shall bring the water out of the rock for them and give drink to the congregation and their cattle.

And Moses took the staff from before the Lord, ad he commanded him. Then Moses lifted up his hand and struck the rock with his staff twice and the water came out abundantly and the congregation drank and their livestock. And the Lord said to Moses and Aaron, "Because you did not believe in me to uphold me as holy in the eyes of the people of Israel, therefore you shall not bring this assembly into the land that I have given them".

James 1:19-20 (ESV) reads, "Know this, my beloved brothers: let every person be quick to hear, slow to speak, slow to anger; for the anger of man does not produce the righteousness of God."

Guilt or Blame

I have done this a million times. Whenever I looked back at my past, I would say, "Surely God must be punishing me." I have begged, bargained and cried to God to remove the pain, the scorn, the shame and humiliation of divorce, to no apparent avail. I have lost count of how often I have cried, "Oh God, what did I do? Is it me?" I have asked myself multiple questions – "What I did? What I did not do? What I should have done?"

When I was having trouble in my marriage like any child of God, I became proactive in trying to fix it. I fasted, "sowed seed" and even named my seed "the restoration of my marriage." I prayed, cried, gave, carried my cross, gave birth to a son and still fell short of recapturing my husband's heart. I prayed all those restoration verses with our names in them, and "confessed a great marriage and a great husband", but nothing changed. I ended up believing that all those curses of divorce and unhappy homes are following me. I cried, "Oh, please God, take the curses away. Is it me who needs deliverance from what is destroying my marriage?"

I had my hair the way he wanted, my face was made up the way he preferred, and my clothes and car were what he wanted me wearing and driving, yet I could not satisfy him. I cried more, "God, what did I do? Is it me?" I cried to God because I felt inadequate. I felt not good enough for him. I felt not tailored for him. I kept asking myself, "How could anyone who felt, looked and smelled so right be so wrong. Is it me?" I did everything according to the book. I waited to get married. I waited to have a child in marriage. At the beginning of our marriage, we did not have a car or a house. We started from nothing, and now we had everything, yet he still broke my heart. I cried more, "God, what did I do? Is it me?" I felt guilty that it did not work because of me.

"Is it me or was it me?" That is a question you will ask yourself multiple times in your journey. How you answer this question will determine the journey to your healing. Though I accept my role in our marriage break-up, I refuse to take the blame for what someone else did, said and decided. It is not my fault that I was insulted, neglected and ignored. It was not my fault that I was not loved. These facts freed me from a lot of "Is it me?" questions. For the longest time I carried the burden of my broken marriage until it came to a point where I laid down that unnecessary burden of guilt and blame by saying, "It was not only me."

Do I wish we did things differently? Yes of course. I wish we had left no stone unturned in seeking solutions to our troubled marriage. We spoke to everyone who could have helped us then, but be it as it may, I reached a point where I chose not to carry that burden on my shoulders any more.

I am naturally not a fighter. I have only recently started learning to fight. Now, I fight for my relationship with my family, with my friends, and mostly with my son. If I get married again, I will surely fight. This is what I tell married people now - fight with all you have to save that marriage, because it will take all that you have to save your marriage. It will take all that you are to make it work!

Guilt was an emotion or rather a phase I went through right after hurt, pain, disappointment and shame. I must say, guilt was a rather surprising emotion for me to experience and go through, because it was so unexpected. I often asked myself why I was feeling that way. I mean, I neither cheated nor were disloyal. I did not take an inappropriate picture with another man. I did not buy a man other than my husband clothes. I did not neglect my home. I did not buy clothes or expensive suits with money I was supposed to use for the family's sustenance. I did not leave my family hungry. So why did I feel guilty?

My guilt was threefold:

1. I felt guilty, because I wanted the divorce, initiated it and went through with it. I brought this to our lives. That is what is in the public domain with my divorce - that I wanted it, yet no one knows how many times I was threatened with divorce until I filed. Actually, I lost count. "You are the one that filed", is the line that many use to impute blame and not take responsibility for their part. By the way, this will come up a bit, if not all the time when divorce or anything to do with it is brought up. Some partners, even if they cheated multiple times, will always remind you that you are the one who filed. Families and friends will be bombarded with, "She is the one divorcing me", or "She is the one who wants the divorce." I initiated the divorce and realized that it was not what I honestly wanted, but my ex-husband went ahead and continued with it. I was relieved that God knew exactly what was going on regardless of how many lies were out there.

I truly did not see guilt coming, because for me, the marriage ended, because my husband did whatever he did and guilt introduced me to my part - the part that I played.

2. I felt guilty for my part in the divorce - at least for initiating it, and I carried that for a long time. I have since come to realize that whether that was the reason for the divorce or not, guilt lets you know that you had a part to play and you have to own up. No marriage is ended by one partner - it is ended by two people.

When I got over the guilt, I was no longer ashamed of walking around town, despite the stares and pointing of fingers by critics. You see, I was married to a Pastor and thus known around our city. So, when we got divorced, it was a scandal, and walking around was not comfortable in the beginning. When the guilt manifested later, I was already over my feelings of shame and embarrassment. Humiliation attacked me, because of what I assumed people thought of me, but guilt was my response to their seeming disgust.

I was compelled to look at myself honestly and admit that indeed I also had a hand in my marital break-up. I felt guilty, because upon reflecting back on my marriage, I had screamed, shouted, gotten angry and sometimes acted irrationally. For these, I was guilty. I sometimes wondered if they were not the causative factors to the ultimate marital collapse, but I did not ask my husband if they really were. It should be appreciated that all these emotions and suppositions I mused over, I could not discuss with him, because I knew I was guilty of a lot of "the little foxes that ruin the whole vine." (Songs of Solomon 2:15)

3. Guilt introduced me to the woman I had become in my marriage. I was a bitter, sad, lonely and mostly fearful woman, and now that she was now staring me in the face, I did not want to ever acknowledge her. I looked into the proverbial "mirror on the wall" and thought, "That can't be me I am seeing there." I had to watch as scenes played out in my mind and I realized then that I was not as innocent as I had assumed. I so cried at this realization and for a while there had a pity party.

I had to deal with the fact that though I had considered myself to be a strong, intelligent and loving woman, I could not be a successful wife. I had failed as a wife. Wives are supposed to be "submissive, quiet and respectful", yet I was plagued by questions such as, "Maybe I don't know how to be submissive or to speak." There were a lot of "maybes" which flooded my mind and burdened my emotions. I was shattered for a minute there! Okay, it was for an hour or maybe a day! I felt guilty for not holding it together as a woman. I often wondered how others did it.

I had conversations with close friends on how I eventually saw how wrong I had been in my marriage. I always wanted to speak and speak the loudest, and if you did not do what I thought you should do, I considered that disrespectful. I wanted us to think alike and do things alike. I could not allow my husband to lead, because I was afraid that he would lead us astray. I trusted no one but me. I was married to him, but I could not be vulnerable enough to voice my fears. I voiced my disagreements, but stayed silent on what went on in my head and heart. I can honestly say that we divorced without ever me sharing my intimate desires, thoughts and dreams with him. I was guilty of not spelling it out to him. I wanted him to sniff it out and when he did not, I considered him not man enough.

After realizing my part in the marriage break-up, I wrote a letter to my husband to apologize. I did not know how much pain I had caused him. I still don't know, but I had to apologize for it all. You can only chip on a stone for so long before it breaks, and most couples don't know how much chipping they are doing to their spouses - the kind of chipping that leaves emotional marks and scars. It is obvious that a man's ego and sense of dignity are impacted negatively by a divorce. So, I admitted to him that knew that I did not let him be the man that God intended him to be. I was in no way saying he was a perfect husband or he did not contribute towards bringing us to the point of marital disintegration. I was merely apologizing for my part in the marital breakdown.

There are times when you have to ask God for forgiveness for things that you did, and there are times when you have to face those you wronged and ask for their forgiveness. You should never be too proud to apologize - it is not humiliating, but shows humility. I had to release myself from the burdens of guilt and offence in order to be free to face the present and the future. I wanted nothing to tie me down to my twisted past, and though I lost nothing by apologizing, I gained total freedom from guilt and shame.

After sending a letter of apology to my ex-husband, I continued praying and waited for his response. Instead of the anticipated response from him, I heard to my dismay, that my ex-husband had told the entire congregation that I was miserable and seeking his attention. Little did he know that while he spread such gossip, I was basking in the presence of God and not in the least interested in justifying my actions and convictions. I resolved to affirm my trust in God who is my Defense;

God who fights my battles, takes care of my needs and to whom my life belongs. I chose to rest in God, my Redeemer - after all, vengeance is His, not mine. Unlike my ex-husband, I did not have the advantage of access to the pulpit to share my stories, but I had my throne room to attend to daily with the King of kings. The throne room is far bigger than any platform.

I resolved not to be bothered with trivialities such as gossip, as they were by far minor compared to what God was doing in my life. So, from that moment I resolved to rest my case and surrender to God completely, for He is forever faithful and just to forgive us if we confess our sins. Beyond that point, guilt left me and I have since never looked back with any interest in reengaging my past guilt, condemnation, shame and embarrassment. I was free to stand before God and praise Him from a pure heart, with nothing else mattering.

It is written in 1 John 1:8-9, "If we say we have no sin, we are deceiving ourselves and the truth is not in us. If we confess our sins, he is faithful and just to forgive us our sins and to cleanse us from all unrighteousness."

Abandonment

Desertion may seem trivial to a lot of people who have not gone through divorce. Some may wonder why I felt abandoned or deserted. Well, we made vows by saying, "I forsake all and I will do life with you regardless of what happens; through thick and thin, through pain, joy, sickness, poverty and all other things we did not plan"; and then you want to bail out after all that? The person who was supposed to love you the most, accept, support and be loyal to you wants to jump ship.

I will give you a bit of my story. I was married to a man who was a "Foreign National" in South Africa; a Ghanaian, which in itself came with a lot of burdens and baggage. There was always that "foreigner" stigma that one carried around for marrying such a man. Some people assumed that you got together with him, because of his money. Far from those assumptions, truth is that when we started dating, we both did not have much. I was working and he was doing ministry full time, so we were not together because of finances. The first year of our marriage, we walked a lot, because we did not have a car and had no furniture at all back home. Our rented house had such an echo because it was empty.

When I told them at home that I am getting married to him, "world war" erupted within the Choene household. My family would not accept this man. I fought tooth and nail for him to be welcomed into this family and almost lost them over it.

I had a wedding and my entire family were present. That is a blessing to any bride, because, honestly speaking, it would have broken my heart if any of my family did not attend. I will forever thank them for putting themselves second by coming. It should then be imagined how I felt at realizing that after all the fighting for him to be accepted and ultimately convincing my family to, it ended in divorce.

As the marriage progressed, my family began to open up and accept him; treating him like part of the family. In fact, he was more of family than I; but then after positive developments, he left me out to dry. I felt like my family was justified in their initial reservations. I felt that after my campaigning for his acceptance, when time came for him to fight for our marriage, he did not man up. I wanted him to fight for me and for us, but he did not. So, yes, I felt abandoned by the one person I was supposed to be close to and vulnerable with.

I felt that he left me out to dry up. It was supposed to be our fight against the world, not us against each other. So, yes, I felt abandoned. Abandonment did not even start when I left our home to file for divorce. I was abandoned way before then. I was left alone way before I left. My leaving was just the next best step. My husband was hardly home. I have felt cold nights before. I have seen empty tables. I have heard and seen closed doors before. I have witnessed empty fridges and cardboards. I have cried alone with no one to hold me tight. I have screamed at empty spaces and deaf ears. I have endured being alone while I was supposed to be with him. So, abandonment started way before the divorce papers were served. With papers served, this abandonment became more real and obvious.

There is hope if we can still fight. There is hope if we can still be in the same room or house. There is hope if we are still in the same car; as you still call me yours. There is hope when you can send messages. There is always hope when we are willing to fight for our marriage. Hope dies the moment someone jumps ship, because jumping ship is enough proof that hope is now dead. The Bible says, "Nothing is impossible with God and nothing is impossible to him who believes." I had lost all belief and did not have hope that anything could be salvaged. That is the worst place for anyone to be, especially one who wants to work things out.

A disconcerting realization hit me - hope is lost only when fellowship with the Holy Spirit and the Word of God are gone. We lose hope at the point we no longer trust God with our lives. While I felt abandoned by man and shamed by many, what freed me was the story of Jesus Christ from Matthew 27: 47, which many refer to as "the fourth word on the cross." It reads thus, "And about the ninth hour, Jesus cried out with a loud voice saying 'Eli, Eli lama sabachthani?' That is my 'God my God why have you forsaken me?'" That was a cry of agony at being betrayed by Judas Iscariot, denied by Simon Peter, not once, but thrice and being abandoned by the other nine disciples. Yet, Christ recovered from the ordeal.

Prior to the suffering on the cross, Jesus Christ had experienced man's betrayal before, yet it did not sting as bad as the day His Father turned His back on Him. Prior to that day, Jesus was always with His Father, did everything after spending endless nights in prayer before the Father; as they were always in communion and fellowship, but as He hung on the cross, it was the first time ever in Scripture we saw Him and the Father not together. That hurt Jesus deeply. His cry is evidence of His realization of being betrayed.

My freedom came when I realized that Jesus' anguish was such as I would never ever experience, as it was mere man, not God, who had abandoned me. I realized that contrary to what Lord Jesus suffered; God would never forsake me despite how people treated me. I realized that I would never be without God. At that moment I realized that though I was abandoned by man, Lord Jesus had neither left nor forsaken me. I still had Him in my life. I realized then that a feeling of abandonment was just that - a feeling; not my truth and reality.

In my time of need, Lord Jesus was right there within and besides me. In that moment, I realized that nothing and no one mattered more to me than He did.

Hebrews 13:5-6, "Keep your life free from the love of money and be content with what you have, for he has said, "I will never leave you not forsake you". So, we can confidently say 'The Lord is my helper, I will not fear. What can man do to me?"

Regret

No amount of regret changes the past.

I have had front row seats to watch a few people go through divorce before. I have seen the patterns go exactly the same way. When one is hit with divorce, a few things always seem to take over. People spiral out of control. I have seen people who hated liquor suddenly become alcoholics. I have seen people who hardly went out become club hoppers. I have witnessed teetotalers become wild party animals that dance on tables and are suddenly the life of the party. They always make a reference to the fact that they are now free to do whatever they please.

The truth is that they are far from being free. The freedom they suddenly feel leads them into habits and decisions that give them a false sense of escapism from their pain. It is both possible and reasonable after a divorce to go out and do things you always wanted to do. When I was in the process of divorce, a friend took me to the movies so that I could get my mind off things. I only realized then that I had not been to the movies in years. That was a reasonable refresher and response to my new found freedom, not the outrageous outlet of anger, rage, pain, bitterness and frustration I referred to in the preceding paragraph.

When I found myself suddenly free, I was literally clueless over how to fill the void of being single again. I thought - now that there are no husband, house and marriage to look after, how do I preoccupy my mind with other activities? I remember lying in bed at one o'clock in the afternoon still in my pajamas. I did not want to go anywhere except to the loo for the occasional forced visits. I did not want to do anything. I had neither energy nor will at all to be re-socialized. During one of my daytime slumber sessions, my older brother came over to my mom's house for a visit. He repeated what he had occasionally told me in the past, which only resonated in me now. He said, "I would rather see you in this condition than any other way." He said, "Cry, be depressed, feel the pain, be as low as you can be, because being any other way would be very alarming to me."

He continued, "How you present is normal behaviour under the circumstances and I would be terrified if you acted any other way. When you are at your lowest, you have no other way but up. As for when the 'up' happens, nobody knows, but I can guarantee you it shall happen." In my deepest pain I saw and felt hope flood my soul. Even though it was for a moment, I nonetheless held on to it. I still cried. I still felt the pain, and though I knew it would ultimately end, I wanted it to end then.

I had many opportunities to medicate my pain. I had other men present themselves as the next best man in my life. Financially and in other regards, some were far better than my ex-husband, but I knew it would be "self-medicating" if I fell for them. I had opportunities to travel in an attempt to numb the pain. I had opportunities to do things out of the ordinary. I had several opportunities of owning cars, having jobs, money and relationships, but I knew it would all be fake. So, l let myself feel the pain. I cried when things reminded me of "us". I cried when nothing reminded me of anything. I cried at watching a famous TV Programme, "Our Perfect Wedding". I cried at hearing love songs, because they reminded me of my loss; but I still refused to self-medicate.

As a child of God, I had no words to pray and no verses to recite. I knew many of them, yet in my distress, I remembered none. When others reminded me of them, I didn't want to hear. I wanted my happy marriage happy back (was it ever happy?). I wanted my dream marriage, not a scripture. Often all I could whisper was "Jesus! Jesus!" endlessly. Other times I would hear my mom pray for me. Sensing the agony in her voice would so break me down and reduce me to tears. I knew she was carrying my pain, yet I refused to self-medicate.

I had offers to move on and enjoy life, yet I still refused to self-medicate. Sometimes I would go out with my friends when laughter and jesting were the order of the day, yet as soon as I walked through that door back home, I was reminded of the pain. Even then, I refused to self-medicate. I knew sex was not the answer, yet others used it to self-medicate. I knew alcohol was not the answer, yet others used it to self-medicate. I also figured out that entertainment was not the answer, though many had resorted to it as a means to self-medication; to numb the pain. After all, numbing is not necessarily therapeutic, hey? Once one resorts to only numbing the pain momentarily, one realizes that there are always triggers in almost all daily activities and moments which bring it back.

There was a point when I used social media to self-medicate. I would post my photos online in an attempt to show the world that I was okay, while deep within me I knew I was not. Then, every Facebook comment and like were like an adrenaline rush to me. I posted status to proof that I was well and kicking, yet I knew I was hurting inside. When I realized how shallow I had become, I stopped self-medicating on social media. I basically refused to self-medicate any longer, because I knew it was going to delay my healing process. So, I took my brother's advice and allowed myself to feel the pain, the humiliation and shame until genuine healing began manifesting.

What you do to heal, matters.

I remember Moruti Shimmy Kotu asking me if I was depressed and I said "Yes". I then honestly told him I didn't even know how I would make it through another day, let alone come to church on Sundays. Daily he would ask me in the morning if I am awake and I would answer, "Yes, Moruti I am." This went on for a week and after a week I started saying it to myself, "I am awake, I am alive, and that pain did not kill me." I repeated it daily until one day I woke up without thinking of the pain, but of being awake and grateful. I would think each morning, "I am alive and I am grateful I am. This can only mean that the Sovereign God wants me here and if anybody else does not approve, shame on them. I am here and I will be happy being here."

Please do not attempt to self-medicate after or during a divorce, because it will only hurt you. I have seen great people self-destruct, because they changed who they were to run away from their pain. For a while it seemed to be working while long term it either stunted their recovery or they destroyed their own lives and every prospect of moving beyond the pain. Some people become workaholics in an attempt to escape the pain, which further alienates them from reality.

After realizing that I was alive and upon developing appreciation for living, I found it easier to return to praying. I had to cast my burdens upon God. This helped me focus on my source of joy and strength instead of fixating on the pain. I began focusing on what God did for me and what He wanted me to achieve through my existence on earth. At that realization, my response to His purpose for my life was a resounding "Yes". I declared, "Lord, have your way in my life." This I said with tears running down my cheeks, but through the tears I had hope once more; hope that God would use me and my life to His glory.

John 11 made me cry so much for as often as I read it. John 11:4, "But when Jesus heard it, he said, 'This illness does not lead to death. It is for the glory of God, so that the Son of God may be glorified through it'".

2 Corinthians 7:9, reads, "As it is I rejoice, not because you were grieved, but because you were grieved into repenting. For you felt a godly grief so that suffered no loss through us. For godly grief produces a repentance that leads to salvation without regret; whereas worldly grief produces death."

Fear

I had fear after the divorce - fear of raising my son by myself. That was my biggest fear, because I had resolved that he would grow up with both loving parents in the same house. I was fearful that he would not be the man he needed to be as a result of growing up in a broken home. I was fearful of how our divorce would affect his outlook on life. I was fearful that his own marriage would be without a good example of parents demonstrating and modelling "till death do us part."

I never wanted him to have to choose between his dad and I, because we are equally his parents. That is the reason I tell him daily that I love him. I tell him that his daddy always loved him. I had to tell him that our being apart was neither indicative of our lack of love for him nor his fault. I still tell him that both mommy and daddy wanted him to be born and his birth was the highlight of our life together.

I always tell him how happy his daddy, mommy and family were to have him. I do not tire from letting him know that he is the greatest gift Lord Jesus gave his daddy and I. I let him know that I am glad he is in my life and how an incredible and amazing individual he is to have on earth. I let him know that he does not owe us anything but love and respect. I tell him that he should not be afraid to be himself and if at any point he feels fearful to be himself, that should prompt him to return to Lord Jesus, who is the reason we live.

I was fearful of my new life. I was no longer in the couples' chat groups, as I had to return to the single group. I did not know how to be in this single group anymore. I did not want to be in this group. When I uttered marital vows, I secretly rejoiced that I had mastered dating and was finally married. How could I have to date again? Now I have to do it again? Like what? Wait I am single once more?

I cried my socks out, because I did not know it would be so hard to accept that my marriage was over and I was single again. I did not know what to do with the "single" title and life. I used to have a permanent date for every occasion, now suddenly I had to rock up alone at events. I was not ready for that. I left the dating scene when my stomach was still flat and had no stretch marks. Now I had a belly, stretch marks and a "C - Section" scar. I now had a son; someone who called me "mommy."

I never wanted to have a baby before getting married, because I did not want to have a protruding belly, stretch marks, a "C - Section" scar and someone calling me "mommy" without a husband! I wanted babies only when I was married, but now, after all those noble decisions I made and kept to, I had a son with no husband. Like Job in the Bible, what I feared the most had befallen me.

Imagine this - every time you meet a new man, you have to disclose that you have a son. Imagine that relationship flourishing and he takes you home to his family and they have to learn that she comes with the burden of another person; a tiny one for that matter. That has always been my worst nightmare. Hence, for all those things I have to think and do, I have completely abandoned all dating prospects. I do not know how or ever want to anymore. For crying out loud, dating has changed. The rules are no longer the same and I choose not to participate in this new game anymore. I am out and I am out forever. I have always been fearful to do life alone; now I do not have a choice! I have to. Above all these psycho-emotional challenges I have to deal with, now another life depends upon me while I often have to admit I do not know what I am doing.

Fear has the ability to preoccupy your mind to a paralyzing extent. I remember driving along National Route 1 (N1) shortly after my separation. A thought struck me as I found myself musing over who I would call in the event of an emergency (breakdown or accident).

Whereas in the past I took it for granted that my husband would come out to help me, I knew that I was now on my own. Such are the paralyzing effects of fear. I am made to believe that according to the Bible, God commanded "Fear Not" 366 times.

If you yield to fear you shall never recover, progress and grow beyond your setbacks - you shall not survive misfortune. I made a choice to trust God regardless of my fears. I chose to trust Him who created the future. Since then, being alone does not scare me anymore. I may be single and on my own and that would still be perfectly fine with me. I refuse to fear for my life just because I am not a "Mrs."

Presently, matters of eternity are a far and greater hope to me than a spouse. I enjoy God's presence so much now and look forward to being with Him eternally. From the lips of Lord Jesus Christ, we learn that despite our present marital status, heaven awaits us, where, by the way, there is no marriage. So, I have decided I might as well enjoy Jesus now, because eternity awaits me to continue gazing into His face forever.

Fear is proof that you have not yielded your life to the Lord. Fear is proof enough that you want to be in control of every little aspect of your life. Fear is proof enough that you don't have faith in God, because faith in God requires you to walk blindly into the future, believing and trusting that God knows everything about it and shall see you through. Faith is leaning fully on the Son of God and his goodness. Fear totally disappears when we have faith in God.

Forgiveness

I SHALL BE THE FIRST to admit that I do not deserve the forgiveness of God. So, to move on, I had to totally repent for the divorce. I had to recognize that I did that which God hated. My heart's desire has always been to please Him, but I could not do that when it came to my divorce.

I always considered myself to have had a bevy of pursuers prior to my marriage. So, much of my regret came from realizing that I had not taken my best option, hence the subsequent marital breakdown. Much as I felt this way, I also gave thought to the possibility that my failed marriage was destined to have happened, except for the wrong turn it took.

On hindsight, I honestly have to admit that there were always red flags in our premarital journey which I completely ignored, thinking we could resolve them. Though you see glaring character flaws in him, you hope that God will transform him and turn him into the man of your dreams. We are not talking superficial flaws such as a poor choice of clothing or a bland fashion taste, but serious issues of character - temper, a roving eye, lack of etiquette and other grievous behaviours you keep sweeping under the carpet, hoping not to find them there the next day.

People always say, "You were blinded". The question becomes, who blinded me? Was it the love, the lover in me or the beloved who blinded me? I think people always choose not to see the obvious and only honestly open their eyes when divorce looms. After we had been in consultation and counselling with parents, pastors, professionals and friends, all in an attempt to seek a resolution to our marital challenges, my husband decided it was enough. He felt he had had enough counselling to last him a lifetime and what should be should just happen.

Since then, I always had nagging thoughts - that I could have done more. Even though that could be true, I had to let go and let what should be just happen. At some point or another, I felt like I was letting everyone down - firstly God, then my son, my mom, my siblings, the entire church and unbelievers who perceive the church as a bunch of losers fooling themselves. I felt like I was adding to the list of what they would point as pretentious and impractical with church life. As it were, I was already the talk of town. Expectations on my marriage working out were high, but thus far, the delivery was so low and we were heading for a divorce.

Further compounding the challenges was the fact that the love supply back home was low, but in public I had to pretend that the love was overflowing. I still cringe sometimes, when I sit around with my family and deep down, I am sad that I brought them so much shame and embarrassment. You see, with a wedding and marriage, you bring them so much joy, but with a divorce surely you are bringing them so much shame and pain. I cannot even imagine the questions they had to answer, because I was not at home to answer to every inquisition by neighbours, relatives and acquaintances. I cannot imagine the looks they had to endure because of my decision. So, somehow it breaks my heart to think about them. They did not ask for it. They were only part of it by virtue of being my family.

I remember having to find a new church. Bloemfontein is not a big city, so I had to endure the humiliation of some pastors preaching about my misfortune, using my marriage and divorce as examples in sermons and pastors' training lectures. So, when a pastor is training their members they would say, "Do not be as disrespectful to your husbands as Kea…" I mean, you are no longer addressed or named as "Pastor Kea", because you are divorced and no longer entitled to that status.

I remember saying to a friend, "Why kick a sister when she is already down?" I could not attend church for a while in Bloemfontein, because I first had to forgive them before I fellowshipped with them. Their words cut deeper than the divorce itself, because I thought church was a place of healing and restoration. I thought if they could not wrap their arms of love around me then, where would I go? I had to make a distinction between God and "church"- that God was not necessarily those that claimed to represent Him.

Throughout all these challenges, I had to forgive everyone I thought or even suspected had wronged me. It was a long process, but I had to. Forgiveness freed me from being bitter, resentful and stressful. Forgiving others freed me from anger and resentment.

Colossians 3: 13 (ESV) reads, "Bearing with one another and, if one has a complaint against another forgiving each other as the Lord has forgiven you, so you also forgive."

There is always a temptation to say, "I want to forgive myself", but there is nothing like that in the scriptures. If I offended anyone I need to go to that individual and ask for forgiveness and if I have sinned against God, then I will ask God for forgiveness. Both those steps should free one from condemnation.

If your partner brings someone in your marriage, you have to forgive them. Even if they end up marrying them and not ask for forgiveness, you still have to forgive them. You have to forgive someone even if they are not remorseful. Even those who insulted and disrespected you have to be forgiven, if you are to move on a free soul. You have to release them from your heart if you are to continue walking peacefully and meaningfully with God. It takes forgiveness to release them and, in the process, release yourself from the offence. We did not deserve God's mercy, grace or forgiveness; neither did we earn them, but He forgave us nonetheless.

Emotions

Emotions are as unstable as the waves of the sea.

In the beginning of the divorce I often cried myself to sleep, because I would play the same memories over and over again in my head to the point of talking myself to sleep over them. The more I mused over them the more I felt down and out. To spoil my good mood, all I had to do was yield to the negative thoughts over my marital demise.

Yes, I was hurt and deeply so, but looking back now, there was no point in mourning that long. Mourning long for the living is deadly, especially if the one you are mourning over is out there having a good time. Talking about them brought some relief, but not too much as it started bordering on idolatry. It was man, not God after all, I had broken up with.

It is true that how you think about things matters and what you tell yourself about things matters more. I cried so much, because of the lies I heard about me on the streets; lies told by my ex-husband. It was painful, but I had to get over it. I had to stop mourning and move on.

I realized then that a part of me was dying. As I have mentioned in the previous pages, no one gets married to get divorced. I had a choice to cry over the demise of my marriage forever or accept that I now had a new life ahead without him. Though I was not certain of what the future would bring, I had to look forward to it. I was not certain what leaving behind everything and moving towards the new meant, but I wanted it with every fiber of my being. I knew without a doubt that the past had nothing for me, so I had to stop mourning and stop it fast.

Mourning is allowed. In fact, it is necessary, but mourning too much is insane and borderline madness. Friends and family can handle mourning for a certain period, but soon you shall be expected to get over it. Too much mourning leads to isolation, because all you ever talk about is what you have lost. Soon this begins to put people off. If all you talk about is your failed marriage, when you come over to visit, people begin to whisper at each other, "Here comes failed marriage", not because they are being mean, but because you have mourned too much. As you discuss your failed marriage, choose wisely who you talk to, because not everyone wants to be an audience to your misery.

We all know that parties are fun, but if they drag for too long, they are a bore. So is mourning; especially mourning over a broken marriage. I know our learned friends - psychologists, psychiatrists and social workers, will say everybody handles pain and loss differently, but trust me on this one - too much mourning is madness which I advise you not to indulge.

I have learned to pray about everything and I have learned to pray in all circumstances. I have learned to pray through various emotions, and I confess to you now that the hardest days to pray are the mourning days; mostly because one struggles to figure out words to utter. Mourning is such that you are focused on nothing else but yourself and do not recognize anything around you. Mostly, you feel like everyone should also shed a tear in sympathy, yet someone who is not in your shoes cannot pull out the mourning feeling on a whim just because you feel emotional.

What helped me tremendously during my emotional days was the advice I received from Pastor Shimmy Kotu. He said, "Do not neglect fellowship, because fellowship with the Holy Spirit is wonderful and fellowship with others can help you." That helped me. I surrounded myself with love and laughter. Divorcees come out of their marriages beaten up. I was practically dead when I left my marriage. I could not recognize who I was anymore. I just went through the motions. I often looked at this girl in the mirror and wondered how she got there. You give so much of yourself to someone and receive nothing in return. You then wonder if the investment was important. I felt like I had invested in this marriage all by myself. I was verbally abused, emotionally isolated and completely unappreciated. As a result, I developed insecurities, bad habits, and other coping mechanisms. I thought I had to save myself, but only realized when it was over that it caused me immense emotional harm from which I needed healing and restoration.

How you feel can be attributed mostly to what you think; so, I had to deal with what I thought and my emotions followed suit.

Making Choices

Divorce left me wondering if I should just lie low and vanish out of my social circles until I had recovered or show up too much in an attempt to show I wasn't that devastated. You know people who show up too much? They are suddenly at every social event, especially those who necessarily did not attend such before their divorce. They are now the ones painting the town red, purple and orange every single weekend. Post-divorce behavioural patterns are important to observe, because others resort to coping habits instead of dealing with their true emotions.

A good day is when the body, soul and spirit are aligned. A bad day is when the spirit wants to get up and go, but the mind and body do not want to cooperate. This is where choices are made daily. I have learned not to rely on my own emotions, because they are unreliable. We all know someone who is happy because they have money and then utterly sad because there is no money. So, emotions are not reliable at all. Half of our issues are solved by choosing to start our day speaking to the One who knows all things and end our day with Him. Choose to walk in a manner worthy of the Lord who has called you. You have to daily choose the fruit of the spirit.

Galatians 5:16 - 18, 22 - 23 reads, "But I say walk by the Spirit and you will not gratify the desires of the flesh. For the desires of the flesh are against Spirit, and the desires of the Spirit are against the flesh, for these are opposed to each other, to keep you from doing the things you want to do. But the fruit of Spirit is love, joy, peace, patience, kindness, goodness, faithfulness, gentleness, self-control, against such things there is no law. "Colossians 1:10 commands us to "Walk in a manner worthy of the Lord, fully pleasing to him; bearing fruit in every good work and increasing in knowledge of God."

Will I Remarry?

The never-ending question I get asked is, "Will you remarry?"

Shortly after divorce, most of us always say we will never ever get married, but mostly our answers or responses are pain and disappointment speaking. For a while I did not have to think about the answer, but the question kept coming up. So, I thought it expedient to answer it for my own sake, just to unlock the puzzle in my head regarding remarriage.

I am an ambassador for marriage. I don't ever think the initial and most convenient option for struggling couples is divorce. So, I do not necessarily have anything against marriage. What I find hard to believe is the existence of an honourable man out there. I have not met enough couples whose marriages are such that I should regret getting divorced. From observation, I am of the opinion that we do not have a lot of husbands who are willing to protect their own families - their wives' hearts and their children's legacy.

So, my desire has always been for an honourable man who will keep his word to me, a man who will protect our relationship; a man who will consciously build himself up, build me up and raise children with me. I am looking for a man who will be a role model in speech, conduct and character to our children; a man who will be a great provider for us, one who will ensure that I live my dreams and won't remain hidden under his shadow.

I need a man who will pray for us, pray with me and pray with our children; a man who will lead our family devotions - one who will gladly share the Word of God with his family. I need a man who will not bail out of his vows when the going gets tough. I dream of a man who when he dies, I will say, "Here lies a man who loved me and loved our children. Here lies a man who was a husband of note and an incredible father; a great provider, an awesome protector, a brave builder of a great name and legacy, an honourable man to me - my hero and champion." If such a man ever crossed my path, yes, I will get married again; but I don't know if he exists.

The toughest factor about divorce and remarriage is the issue of comparison. Some people go for the same version of their ex and others swear to never date such and go for someone completely different. The problem with both scenarios is that your past and your partner still dominate your heart to the extent that they become a point of reference for your future choices and decisions.

What I have learned though is that my worth does not come from being linked to any man. I have learned that even if I die single, I would have still lived a fulfilled life. I have learned that I am a whole person who does not need anyone else to complete. I am not a puzzle with various pieces. I come all glued up together to make it to the other side. I have learned that buying a car, a house and life insurance are not a male thing; neither are they exclusively a married couple's indulgence, as they can be done and achieved by anyone. I am so content on my own that I don't search for my happiness in anyone.

Psalm 139 says, "I am fearfully and wonderfully made." After hearing those words, what could another human being offer me that God Himself has not already provided? I was made complete and the notion that I need someone else before my life can matter, is a lie that wounds and haunts forever; because if I buy into it, I will forever look upon another to validate me. No human being will ever make us whole, happy or satisfied. So, I am super content with Jesus in my life. I live from the inside out and am joyful. All I need to make it to the other side I have.

So, to answer the remarriage question - the man I want does not exist; so, I am perfectly okay with that. Many assume that I daily get home to mope and weep myself to sleep. That is not a fact. Firstly, I have a son who is fascinated by planets, space, rockets and numbers; so, you can imagine how I spend my days. Yes, you guessed it - gazing into outer space. That keeps my mind occupied; seeing how that has never been my interest at all. As he learns, he is teaching me a lot.

Secondly, I am an avid reader. I read things most people have not heard of - very old books. My subjects of choice include human behaviour, sociology, psychology and children's development. I also visit motivational blogs and spiritual upliftment websites. These I consume a lot.

Thirdly, I write for fun. I write when I am sad and I write when I am confused. I write regardless of what I am feeling, thinking or processing in my mind and life - it all somehow ends on a piece of paper.

My other favourite fascination is to help others. I will not disclose what I do though, but I love reaching out. I also love to pray. You cannot pray and feel alone; that is impossible, because the One you pray to has a way of filling your heart and soul with life. How can I feel lonely when I have the greater One living in me? I cannot imagine praying and being lonely, because God has already promised that He will neither leave nor forsake me.

So, my life is neither lonely nor sad, because there is a whole world out there that needs to be explored. I am ready to do it and if anyone ever joins my life as a husband, they will get a fabulous, loving and adventurous woman who has her heart wrapped in Christ's heart.

Hebrews 2:5-6 reads, "For it were not angels that God subjected the world to come of which we are speaking. It has been testified somewhere, what is man that you are mindful of him or the Son of man that you care for him?"

Label

I am often told that I am not good enough for another man to marry. The world shows me daily that I am a failure. We are told we are old and all great men are taken. We are told we will grow old, grey and alone. We are told that we need to accept that we will die alone, especially in church circles. I am reminded of how I am no longer allowed to date and remarry.

When I attend our marriage seminars at church, I cannot help but wonder if I am setting myself up. I wonder if I ever get married, will I be accepted or not? Some folk have already confessed their discomfort at my presence. Some suggest I should forget about remarrying. They have indicated that since remarriage is not in the Word of God, I should not attend the dating and marriage seminars. They have indicated that God does not recognize second marriages and when I remarry, God will not recognize my marriage.

None of these people even know my plans or desires. Here is my point - people driven by prejudice always label others. None of these people know anything about my failed marriage, life or divorce, yet they presumptuously judge me and give uninvited advice. This has happened, continues to happen and I suspect shall continue to happen. The sad fact about it is, the more it does, the more societal prejudices and ill-informed expectations further burden me.

Our worth and value do not rely on man's approval of us. "Divorcee" could be and will be a label that we will carry forever. We are known as the "do not marry bunch." Because we were married before, men are told to stay clear of us. People find the need to tell you how much God disproves of you, even the people we fellowship with weekly. I resolved not to be deterred by such from living the only life God has given me.

I can't speak for everyone and I can't stop anyone from speaking whatever their truth is, but imagine if someone who wanted to marry you felt he was compromising himself. Truth is, it will take a real brother to ignore the "divorcee" label and take the plunge. It is, however sad that people don't realize how hurtful their prejudice is. As it is, divorce is painful enough without all stereotypes associated with it; hence I choose to labour only under my God-given label. Truth is, He loved me enough to send his Son to die for me. So, I am worthy of the love that I receive from Him, by virtue of the sacrifice Jesus became for my sake.

Dating and remarriage are not only about being romantically involved, but about knowing that you deserve to be loved regardless of what others say about you. There are other people in the world who love you - your family, friends and those special people in church. So, be open to receive that love and remove the blinders of hate that others wants to put on you.

It took me time to walk into those marriage seminars with my head held up high, because in the past I always felt I was targeted for ridicule, criticism and censure.

Think on These

I now fully understand why God hates divorce. The extent to which divorce rips your soul apart often feels and seems impossible to repair and heal. Even the healing process leaves some nasty scars. The deep wounds and pain that God's children experience are of a violent nature indeed. God hates divorce, because of the harm and pain it causes the divorcees, their children, their families and their socio-spiritual circles.

The church is likened to the bride of Christ. As a bride, the Church holds on to the hope that no matter what we go through in the world, our Groom, Lord Jesus, will never leave nor forsake us. Our assurance as the church comes from the belief that though gone for a while, Lord Jesus shall soon return for us, His Bride. In the same way, our earthly marriages should model that "never-leaving-nor-forsaking-each-other-despite-what- happens-to-us" relationship we see between Christ and His Church. The vows we make before friends, family and God should be honoured.

Malachi 3:4 reads, "But you say 'Why does he not hear us?' Because the Lord was witness between you and the wife of your youth." God is a witness to our vows and marriages. Every spouse on earth wants to know; in fact, needs to know beyond a shadow of doubt that, "No matter what the circumstances, errors and indiscretions there may be, my spouse will come for me."

What further enhances our confidence in our spouses never leaving us is the truth that when we get married, we become one flesh. Divorce was never God's original plan for us. It is only by virtue of our hardened hearts that it becomes a consideration and option. In your time of despair, brokenness, anger, dejection and confusion, find solace in God. There definitely is no place other than at His feet where you regain your wholeness.

I am often asked what the biggest loss was from my marital demise. Many would recount the loss of money like I did, loss of a home like I did, loss of a car like I did and loss of friends like I did; but I have always honestly told people that in retrospect, I realize that I did not lose much. This response always puzzles everyone, because they cannot imagine how I can make that statement when I do not have much materially. I tell them I did not lose much, because I still have Jesus. I did not lose Him in the midst of it all and He is all I need. He alone will save me through every storm, battle, emotion and beyond the grave.

Yes, my husband, home, cars and money are gone, but everything can be recovered with time. Only Lord Jesus is irreplaceable. He, after all, took my place on the cross and died for my sin though He had never sinned. The One born of a virgin, lay dead in the tomb, was raised from the dead on the third day and ascended to heaven! There is no other God for me but Him.

I do not know what the future holds, but I know who holds the future. There is complete healing and wholeness after divorce. I am a living testimony of that. I hold no grudges, bear no bitterness and feel no hurt, pain or resentment. I hold no unforgiveness, nor do I wish anyone harm or misfortune. I live a life of total freedom in Christ.

Your Life story has not ended just because your marriage has. You have not ended just because your marriage did. Just because one human being on earth has rejected you, does not mean you are not amazingly wonderful. Despite your trials and ordeals, you could come out of this life more beautiful than when you began the journey.

Life could have been different for me today had I not chosen to cry out to God. The best place to be is being broken yet laying prostrate before His throne. He never rejects that broken heart as He wants to put it together again into something brand new. All you have to do is surrender that broken life and give it to Him. Repent of your sins and cry out to Him to save you, for Jesus is the only one who knows how to put you back together and make you whole.

Death and The End

A year has gone by since the divorce and tears have dried up. Life has moved on. The divorce became official on July 17 2017 after we were in separation for a while. My ex-husband got married a month and a week after our divorce, on the 27 August 2017. I could not believe it. Our divorce decree had not yet officially arrived when he was verbalizing his vows to his new wife. The Department of Home Affairs still considered us married and our marital status still reflected "married" when he stood before the Pastor and married his second wife.

On 14 August 2018, exactly a year and 28 days following our divorce, a day which started off as normal ended up in tears and disbelief. A man who had always portrayed strength and health was now lying lifeless in hospital. He was gone! He had died and I was utterly shocked. That day went by with me asking a lot of questions with no answers.

We received the news that death had come and the end was pronounced to the man I once called husband; a man I now shared a precious son with. At first I was shocked and really cried. The crying was both spontaneous and subconscious. I cried for my son who at 6 years old would no longer have a daddy. I cried, because I knew life as we knew it no longer existed. I cannot really state with certainty why I cried and why I was sad, but I was. The reality of oneness struck me again; that ripping apart of my soul recurred. I felt as if a part of me was gone. I had a hard time closing my eyes to sleep, because I could see his face. I saw that face only a day before his passing, when he came to fetch our son for school.

As days went by, I realized how I had previously grieved the same man in the privacy of my own room. I grieved him while he walked this planet. I grieved him while I saw him daily as he came to see his son or took him to school. So, now, when our families and communities mourned his passing on, I realized that I had no grief left for him. The first day of hearing about his death was hard on me. On that very day I had to tell my son he was gone forever. I wanted him to hear it from me. I waited for a few hours before delivering the news and when I finally did, he cried like he had never before.

I had given birth to this boy. I had seen him in painful experiences before, but this was far too much and far too deep. It took me back to the day I learned that my father had died. I had a knot in my heart that I could not remove and I wondered if my son had the same feeling. I could not tell. We could not even have a conversation about it, because, how could I explain that feeling to a six-year-old? The same look I saw the day we left my matrimonial home to return to my mom's home is the same look I look I saw on my son's face. I knew things would never be the same. I could not believe that my ex-husband was gone. As the days went by, I began to receive messages of condolences and deep down I wanted to fly the flag and say. "I did not lose a husband today or yesterday. I officially lost a husband a year ago and I did not receive a phone call from you to wish me strength. All I received were judgmental looks and hostile remarks".

As hours became days and days became weeks, I began to realize how much God had spared, saved and snatched me from an unpleasant experience which could have been ugly now. I made peace with the days that I wrestled with myself asking God about my future. A year ago, I was crying over this man's rejection of me and now I was here crying over his premature death. His death was a shock to me. Even if I had written my own life script, the plot would not have included his death.

As preparations for his funeral were underway and his people asked me if I wanted to say or do something, I said "No." I had no desire to say anything. I desired nothing from the whole experience really. I knew for my son's sake I had to attend the funeral. I figured if ever I wanted to say anything, that could have been when I was married to him. If I ever wanted my voice to be heard, it could have been the years I was his wife. At this stage, anything I ever wanted to say to him was buried a long time ago. I was no longer his wife and I desired to say nothing at his funeral.

I was shocked at the level of hypocrisy displayed. People have more respect of death than they have for life. Suddenly everyone loved him and now loved me so much that they wanted me to toe the line. I plainly refused. I would not join them in their deception.

All I could think of during this time was my son. What gave me comfort was remembering how the Lord had seen me through the humiliation, shame and dishonour my divorce subjected me to and brought me to a place of peace, recovery and healing. I remembered how He put the pieces of my heart together. I recalled how the Lord mended my life in a way no one else could. Consequently, I resolved to entrust my son's recovery to the Lord. Though I did not know how or when He would restore us, I knew He ultimately would.

As the days went by, I was invited to his house. As we walked in, I said to my mom, "The nerve this man had to decorate and design his new house after our old matrimonial home; down to the colour scheme". I secretly laughed and thought, "You lived your old life in your new era. Everything remained the same. You just changed wives."

I looked his wife in the eye for the first time and I said in my heart, "I don't wish to be you right now. I don't wish to have been you since day one." I looked at her and I thought, "Wow! I thought this moment would feel different but it does not." I felt nothing. I travelled back in time to old memories and could not trace one single emotion from the past. I left that house feeling sorry for him and her; regretting every tear I ever shed over him. Sitting in that house while everyone mourned his passing away brought about a realization of how his poor choices led all of us there.

As the days went by, the shock began to wear off. Some people genuinely felt sorry for me. Others avoided me, because they did not know what to say to me. I kept thinking of his death. I used to think his passing on would mean nothing to me, but when I got the news, I cried. I was taken aback by my own reaction and said to friends and family, "I did not think this could affect me at all." I thought, "I had lived the previous two years totally dependent on God and I was not going to go into panic mode now."

Beyond that moment, I felt total freedom; not from anything in particular, but to ultimately move on. For two years prior to his demise, I had witnessed a home I built for so long crumble. Since the divorce, I wrestled a lot with remarrying and moving on, but realized that when it came to relationships I was greatly conflicted.

I remember when I called my friends one day during our divorce and asked them to intercede to God for the restoration of my marriage. I asked them to pray with me. I remember when I fasted and prayed that our marriage be spared, but he still left. I struggled a lot with divorce. I said to God, "I might not think much of this marriage, but to honour you, I will go back." My friends were as confused as I was when our prayers did not yield the desired results. Some thought I was mad to hold on to the hope of reconciliation and others advised that I let go and move on.

It was the hardest period of my life. I could not understand why God in His divine power could not just save my marriage. I begged God and He did not save it. I had no choice but to finally succumb to the reality of it being over. I had to endure the humiliation and the shame of thinking that God had refused to come through for me. I did so much just to save my marriage, but it was too late to salvage the pieces of our broken lives. When he remarried, the reconciliation door was finally shut. I had only one door and one option left - to remain single. I could not do it.

Initially it was easy for me to say, "I do not want to ever remarry", but later I grew extremely uncomfortable with the idea of being alone forever. I have lost count of how often I grieved over it to Moruti Shimmy. I was conflicted, because I wanted to please God, yet I was feeling overwhelmed with despair. People simply said, "Pray those feelings away." I tried, but it seems as if God kept quiet on this. I kept praying about it, for I desperately wanted to accept and embrace my singleness.

I knew that nobody understood what was going on in my head. It is so easy for married couples to say, "Remain single", while they go to bed with their spouses. Some days were better than others. I could not understand why it was so hard to let go. I was basking in the presence of God. I was at the best place ever in my life, yet there was this area called relationship that was just not adding up. I remember thinking, "Jesus is my all. I put Him and His word first, so, why can't I accept this?" I cried to God about it so often.

I thought of what my ex's death meant to me. It meant that I was officially a single parent to my little "bambino." It also meant that I was officially single - no living ex-spouse attached to. I looked into the eyes of my freedom and I smiled. I was now free to be chosen. It was a pity that it was at the expense of someone's pain and sorrow. I was overjoyed that I would no longer have the cloud of "not available" hanging over my head. The idea of freedom was overwhelmingly joyous to think about.

His memorial service was too painful to write about in this book. He was a man, who despite his many errors, loved his son unconditionally. Yet his son was not well represented at this memorial service. If I had to write a message to my ex-husband, Kwame Boakye, for his funeral this would be it –

"Kwame, I can still picture your face as you heard the news that we will be parents. You could not believe that you are going to be a daddy. We found out at 6 weeks and had to keep the news to ourselves with only our parents' knowledge. What a hard secret to keep. You spoke to Nahum before he was even born. You loved him from 6 weeks in the womb until the day you died.

Anyone who knew you, knew you loved Nahum so much. You, Kwame Boakye, were a damn good dad. With you not here, I wonder who will cut Choaro's hair? Who will take him for his vaccinations? Who will take him to school daily? These chores and several other fatherhood tasks I did not have to worry over, because you gladly did them.

In my mind, I imagined you teaching Nahum to drive. I saw you talking to him about girls. I saw you driving him to his graduation, his matric dance and his wedding.

You and Nahum had such a special bond that when you passed on, he felt it in his spirit. He was restless and irritated. When he found out about your passing on, he said "Mommy, how will life be like without daddy?" You, Kwame, were a damn good dad. I told Choaro that, "I do not know how life will be without daddy, but God has our back."

I call Nahum 'Little B', because he is a 'Boakye.' Though we were not together, I wanted him to know where he came from. I will continue to remind him that he is a 'Boakye.' I will continue to remind him that he comes from a family of faith and grace; a family which follows no one but Jesus - a family which prays. That is who he is and where he comes from. Nahum will know that he was greatly loved by his father.

You, Kwame Francis Boakye, were a good dad"

As I saw my son go through this process, I realized that death was much easier than divorce. Family and friends are torn apart during divorce, yet death brings them closer together. Divorce is devastating to a child. My son still remembers how his father and I were during the divorce. I wonder if that picture will ever be erased from his memory. He remembers how lonely his father was and how much I used to cry.

He was always torn between us. He always wondered how the other one was without him. When he had to go to his father's house, he always got sad, because he was leaving me alone. His happiness was always dependent on him being assured that both daddy and mommy were well. He wanted us to get back together. Children are amazing in that they don't see impossibilities like we do. Even after his father was married to someone else, his hope in our reconciliation was never diminished. The dream of his parents getting back together remained alive.

Imagine that tiny soul carrying such a burden. He was aware of how different the cultures were in his dad's home and ours. Divorce was hard on my son. We had to be called in at school, because he was no longer actively participating in his school activities. His father's remarriage led to more meetings at his school, because he could not cope. Divorce was a disaster for him emotionally. I always thank God that he gave me a son that can talk to me.

Death on the other hand was not as devastating to him as divorce. Though he tells me daily that he misses his dad, he mentioned to me the other day that he is glad that he does not have to go back and forth between daddy and mommy; that he now stays in one house. He told me how much we will not have to argue and fight with daddy anymore. He told me that now he can be my son full time.

Divorce and remarriage put children in such a predicament, because they feel they have to please strifing parents and strange step parents. I had no idea that his little heart and mind carried that much burden. I could not believe he processed things to that extent. Truth is, divorce was much harder on us than death.

At his funeral I realised how much they did not know him, because if they did, they would have included so much more than the unnecessary stuff that they put in the programme. Sitting in that funeral service, no fight, argument, job, other woman or organisation mattered. I then realised that what drove us apart was not as important as it seemed then. The people we fought over were no longer that important. I sat there and wondered if we really focused on what mattered. I wondered if our focus was solely on us and our son, would we have lost each other? I had too many questions running through my mind, but I could not have a discussion with him as he was gone and not returning.

As the funeral service ended, I realized how much of a Boakye I still was, even though I had not been one for a while. I felt like them and I was hurting like them. They treated me like their own. I realized then how much divorce had robbed my ex-husband and I. I could not sleep, as I kept wondering how things got to this point. I knew then there was no way I could stop being a part of his family, because I had their grandson; their nephew. The love between the dad's family and my son was undeniable. I could not deprive my son of knowing his father's family.

I looked at his tombstone with disbelief - that a man I once called my husband was lying there. I could not reconcile the two. He was such a picture of strength - that man used to work so hard with his hands and did not rest for a moment, but now he was gone. A man who promised me forever was lying down there. The father of my son was lying there. Sorrow and pain filled my heart. In my wildest dream, I had never imagined this man dying - no I did not.

I looked at his name and I stood in fear of God. I stood in fear of God, because when we first met, he told me how God had told him I was the one. He told me how he prayed for a wife and not only did I have the qualities of a wife but God clearly pointed him to me. I wondered as I stood there if he would have kept to God's leading would he be lying there? I remember how he told me that he could not sleep, because I was on his mind day and night.

My mind went back to the day he told me that he had moved on and I asked him if God changed his mind, and he said a resounding "Yes!" Then I asked him, "Are you certain that God has changed his mind?" He said, "Yes!" I then told him, "Henceforth, I will never bother you again about marriage, divorce or anything to do with us."

I stood there looking at his tombstone and I said, "God, you are in control." I realized then that divorce can mess up your life. I am in no way insinuating anything regarding his death. All I am saying is - God defends marriage, because He is its Creator. No man created it; God did and God at any given moment will defend and protect it. His mind on marriage has not changed. He wants us to be married forever until death do us apart, regardless of what others preach or say. Truth is, God meant it to last forever, yet we are the ones messing up God's order. How do we mess up a plan that we did not come up with? We did not come up with marriage; God did and He knows why He created it. He said "Forever." Let's us not mess up with His blue-print.

I looked at his tombstone and realized that divorce should never have taken place, but it was too late. I was reminded of a verse that I held on for so long when the divorce started, Psalm 46:10, "Be still and know that I am God."

It is the same verse I am holding on to today.

Poem

Saying, 'Goodbye'
When I finally said, 'goodbye'
I looked behind and knew I could never move forward with you.
When I finally said, 'goodbye'
I looked around and knew I could no longer keep you with me.
When I finally said, 'goodbye'
I looked ahead and could not see you in my future.
When I finally said, 'goodbye'
I closed a door that I no longer wanted reopened.
When I finally said, 'goodbye'
I did not have any hellos left in me for you.
When I finally said, 'goodbye'
I no longer had any space for you in my heart.
When I finally said, 'goodbye'
I no longer opened my eyes, wishing you would call.
When I finally said, 'goodbye'
I no longer saw you any more amazing to me.
When I finally said, 'goodbye'
I knew I was better off without your kind.

When I finally said, 'goodbye'
I knew then that your voice would never sound any sweeter.
When I finally said, 'goodbye'
I knew that though your scent would take me back to a place of
pleasure
I wanted to stay in forever-lost-to-me valley.
When I finally said, 'goodbye'
I knew the taste of your once sweet kisses would now taste so bitter.
When I finally said, 'goodbye'
I knew there was someone greater than you out there...

Epilogue

Reasons I am happy that my Marriage Failed and I am out of Institutionalized Christianity

I Wake Up Content

I am glad that chapter of my marriage is closed. I am happy that my marriage ended. I am extremely happy that I left my previous church - "Christ Embassy." It was a place I should not have been and if my marriage did not end, I would probably still be basking in that falsehood. I feel I was snatched from that cult for a reason, because leaving that "church" was the beginning of the deception wearing off. It was like a drug and I had to leave that cult for it to be out of my system and once it was out, I soon realized how toxic it was for me. It took the demise of my marriage to set me free. So, yes, I am glad those two chapters will never be opened again unless in a constructive conversation.

I Am Now Awake

When I left my marriage, I was half dead. The body was well, but the heart, soul and emotions were badly damaged to a point of near death. Today I am that bubbly girl who smiles from her heart, not out of pretence. I look at myself in the mirror and I love who I see. I am no longer in tears, sad and angry. I am so joyful; my loud laugh is contagious even to me. I pass that around and get it right back from those around me.

I Can Now Dream and Pursue Those Dreams

I am a girl who dreams and goes after my dreams now. This book you have in your hand was a dream and here it is now fully manifest. This is just the beginning. When I was invited to be on SKM Radio Network, I could only cry and scream, because that was another dream I had. Here I am, from being told how I should shut up about my dreams and ideas to building again and seeing those same dreams come alive. Radio and Christian Radio in particular, has always been a dream whose fulfilment I often doubted, but here am I now, living it out. I did not go out looking for it, but our paths crossed and we met. And what a joyful ride it has been.

I Am In love With Jesus

I am fully pursuing Jesus, I am in "Pursue Jesus" mode and in that mode I found many other things that I love doing. No one forces me to serve - no threat, curse talk or blackmail. I am willing and obedient. I am not doing it for a men's applause or approval. I am not doing it for awards or to be praised by others. My focus is on Jesus Christ alone. My life's desire is to bring Him glory.

I Look Forward to the Future

I am no longer anxious, apprehensive or doubtful about my future. I look forward to what God has in store for me. I am honoured daily to commune with God who created all things including me. Why should I be sad when I face my days with Him? His Word has become the treasure that I seek, possess and joyfully pass on to others. My days are made, having to wake up to my God.

I Am a Bookworm

I am not the go-shopping type of woman. I buy what I need when I need it. I am a go-and-get-as-many-books-and-read type of woman. So, my days (when not volunteering) are spent behind closed doors, reading and working on my mental muscles. I love reading and spend my days getting into books. I read and meditate on the Word of God, because my life depends on it.

I Get to Be Myself

Institutionalized Christianity can slowly kill who you are, because you have to dress, speak and assume a particular demeanour. If you do not, you are deemed disobedient, not considered part of the collective or authentic enough. If you do not conform to protocol, you are considered not to possess the anointing of "our ministry". I had to fight constantly to be myself at church and at home. I had no voice, because as soon as I spoke up, I was either shunned or chided. I could not even laugh - that is how confined I was. Now I get to speak, laugh and I write what I want. Mostly I get to be myself, have my hair the way I want it, wear what I want and laugh as loud as I can.

I Have My Family

If you come from a place where you could not have a holiday or see your family, because of ministry, you will not understand why I am grateful to have my family. I could not visit my mom who lived 15 minutes away from us. I could not have a meal with my friends or go to family gatherings. I was bound to what they called "service." What type of "service" does not allow for family visits or family holidays? Now I spend all my days talking to my sister, checking up on my brothers and going out with my friends. I do not miss family gatherings or friends' weddings anymore. I am now available for those I love.

I Am Now Intelligent

I no longer have to act dumb for others to shine. I do not have to be dumb for others not to feel intimidated. I speak my mind and ask relevant questions. For the longest time I was told that I speak too much and I must learn to speak less. I was told that I think I know too much. Now I say what I want to say and sound as intelligent as I want. I can be freely pretty and smart now, because for some time I was not allowed or expected to be. Now, like any intelligent person, I do know stuff; you know (laughing out loud!).

I Have a Second Chance

I know for sure that I have a second chance at life. I am now building a solid foundation. The old building was demolished and I had to start afresh. All those wrong decisions that I made on career, relationship and life I now have a chance to correct. I look at my life and my face beams with hope. The structure will be more solid this time around. I am building slowly but surely. Wisdom is at play. I always say now that I am the girl who is not afraid to start all over and I am loving every step of it.

Poem

Eyes
When I looked into your eyes
All I saw was an opportunity of a million memories.
When I looked into your eyes
All I saw were endless possibilities of the unknown.
When I looked into your eyes
All I saw was, 'the past is over and here lies the future.'
When I looked into your eyes
All I saw was, 'this is how it should be done.'
When I looked into your eyes
All I saw was my place to be.
When I looked into your eyes
All I saw was God's greater plan.
When I looked into your eyes
All I saw was, 'welcome home.'
When I looked into your eyes
All I saw was a reflection of me - the me in love.
When I looked into your eyes
All I ever saw was love.
Now, all I know is that I want to gaze
Into those eyes forever!

About the Author

Mom to Choaro Nahum Osei.

Daughter to Ivy Emily Choene.

Sister to Will, Tsholofelo, MacDonald and Moipone.

Aunt to Abongile, Will II and Naledi.

The highest calling for her is being a servant and follower of Jesus Christ.

She is saved by grace and loves much, because she has been forgiven much.

She is a Jesus gal through and through.

She serves the Master who gave His life for hers; the Master who requires nothing less than her life. She surrendered her life to live for His glory. She spends that life pursuing, serving and doing what her Master commands. In Him she lives, she moves and has her being.

She believes that if you love Him, you will tell others about Him, because in the end it is all about Him.

About the Publisher

Published by Shimmy C. Kotu for
Family House Publishers (Pty) Ltd
P.O. Box 21994, Helderkruin, 1733, Republic of South Africa
www.shimmykotu.com
www.familyhouse.co.za
chi@shimmykotu.com